A Simple Guide to Self-Publishing

A Step-by-Step Handbook to Prepare,
Print, Distribute & Promote Your Own Book

Revised Third Edition

A WISE OWL BOOK
www.wiseowlbooks.com/publish

A Simple Guide to Self-Publishing
Copyright © 1994, 1996, 2000, 2003 by Mark Ortman
All rights reserved

6 7 8 9 10 / 2006 2005 2004 2003

Revised Edition: September 2003

ISBN 0-9634699-1-6

Library of Congress Catalog Card Number: 99-96736

Manufactured in the United States of America by Lightning Source, Inc.

WISE OWL BOOKS • Box 29205 • Bellingham WA 98228 • USA • (360) 671-5858

On the Internet: http://www.wiseowlbooks.com/publish

Publisher's Cataloging-in-Publication

Ortman, Mark.
    A simple guide to self-publishing: a step-by-step handbook
to prepare, print, distribute and promote your own book / by
Mark Ortman. -- 3rd ed.
    p. cm.
    Includes index.
    LCCN: 99-96736
    ISBN: 0-9634699-1-6

    1. Self-publishing--United States--Handbooks,
manuals, etc. I. Title.
Z285.5.O77 2000   070.5'93
                                             QBI95-1381

Acknowledgments

A special thanks to the many people who helped make this book possible: Al West for his friendship and continued encouragement, Brian Templeton for his savvy recommendations, Herman Liebelt (in remembrance) for his tireless reviewing and coaching, Cynthia Johnson for contributing her creative talents, Julie Duffy, Jim Patterson and Jeff Young for imparting their wisdom on electronic publishing, to the students who asked the difficult questions and, the members of the local publishing group for sharing their lessons, expertise and support. Finally, a special thanks to all of those who have taken the time to write me their comments, praise and suggestions.

Dedicated to those who are pursuing their dreams.

Contents

Introduction

Self-publishing has become one of the fastest growing segments in the publishing industry today. With a computer, desk top software (such as: Pagemaker, In-Design, Publisher or Quark-X-Press - simple layouts can be produced with Microsoft Word or WordPerfect) and a printer, anyone can publish a book based on a story, expertise or inspiration.

You may have heard success stories of people who self-published and sold tens of thousands of copies. That does happen. However, self-publishing is a risky business and warrants caution. The fact remains, that out of every ten books published, three earn a profit, four break even and the rest lose money. With those odds it is sensible to approach this venture wisely.

No one can predict the commercial success of a book. The only way to find out is to give your idea the best possible chance to succeed with the least risk. To write a book is an art; to self-publish is a business. This is often overlooked until you are stuck with a garage full of unsold books. Your financial risk can be offset significantly by determining if there is a market for your book. Share your manuscript with members of your target audience, and ask them for an honest assessment. Even consider submitting an excerpt from your manuscript to a magazine or newspaper to see what interest is generated. If you are still enthusiastic, print a small quantity and promote your book to see how it sells beyond your friends and family. If it sells, print more; if it doesn't, you are not out a fortune. This is called **test marketing**. Other advantages of testing the water before taking the plunge are making intelligent decisions based on facts, not emotions, keeping your day job until your book proves successful and learning the best ways to promote and sell your book as you find your way around the world of publishing. With the overwhelming nature of the information age, the **purpose** of this book is to be an easy to understand, step-by-step guide to the self-publishing process. Filled with checklists, references, worksheets and money saving ideas, this guide will help you steer clear of the potential hazards of publishing a book on your own. Whether you publish online, print hundreds or thousands of copies, and market them locally or nationally, this book can save you time and money.

The book is organized into five chapters: Getting Started, Printing, Announcing Your Book, Distribution and Creating a Demand (both conventionally and online). There are two indexes at the back of the book: Subject and Organizations. The revised third edition now includes two new ways to publish your book: online publishing and print-on-demand. Also added is an expanded Creating a Demand chapter which includes an updated internet section for promoting your book on the World Wide Web. Internet addresses have been added where available.

Reading this book is a beginning, not an ending. You are urged to add depth to the ideas on the following pages before you make your final decisions. Request information from the many organizations listed, as they provide other useful services beyond the pages of this book. Self-publishing is not a get-rich-quick scheme and requires hard work and perseverance. I now understand why so many people in this industry have courteously uttered these parting words, similar to those often heard in a gambling casino's token window: **"Good Luck!"**

Mark Ortman

Five Reasons to Self-Publish

1. Time. Most royalty publishers work on an 12-18 month production cycle. Do you want to wait that long to get into print? Self-publishing will take 4-9 months (depending on your marketing plans) after completing the manuscript.

2. Control. If you like the final say on the direction of your projects, then self-publishing will give you this freedom. While a royalty publisher's experience and advice may be beneficial, why give a third party the final say if its interests and intentions are different from your own?

3. Ownership. After signing a contract, a royalty publisher owns certain rights to your book, thus preventing you from printing copies when interest declines and your title goes title out of print... unless of course you *purchase* those rights back. A self-publisher owns all the book's rights and may sell all, none or a portion of those rights at any time.

4. Make Money. Why accept a 5 to 15% royalty when you can have a 20-80% *(or more)* margin? Sure, a royalty publisher may have distribution in place and will finance the project, but guess who does all the promoting anyway? If your self-published book proves successful, then you can pursue a royalty publisher and negotiate from a position of strength and experience.

5. To Be In Print. Not everyone publishes to make money. There are several other reasons, such as: seeing your name in print, leaving a legacy to your family or sharing what you have learned with others. Whatever your motive, a book is a personal expression that can lead to new experiences, possibilities and opportunities. A book takes on a life of its own, and you can become a part of that exciting life.

The Three Most Important Questions

Before you decide to publish your own book, be clear as to your purpose. Take time to carefully reflect on these three questions, as the answers will help you make key decisions throughout the publishing process. Refer to page 43.

1. WHY do you want to publish your book?

2. WHO is your audience?

3. WHAT makes your book unique or different?

A journey of a thousand miles begins with a single step.

The secret to writing a best seller is simply having a good book for which there is a need, at the right price, offered to the right market.

1. Getting Started

Learning About the Industry

❏ There are several sources of information to help you learn about the industry. Before embarking on any major project, it only makes sense to familiarize yourself with the lay of the land. Contact the following organizations and publications to request membership information and magazine samples.

American Booksellers Association (ABA)
828 S Broadway
Tarrytown NY 10591
(800) 637-0037
www.bookweb.org

Also request a list of the regional booksellers associations and a sample of the *American Bookseller* magazine.

PMA
627 Aviation Way
Manhattan Beach CA 90266
(310) 372-2732
www.pma-online.org

SPAN
Box 1306
Buena Vista CO 81211
(719) 395-4790
www.spannet.org

These two associations provide co-op membership services to independent publishers.

Publishers Weekly
Box 16178
North Hollywood CA 91615
(800) 278-2991
www.publishersweekly.com

Request a sample copy of the industry's trade journal.

❏ **Visit Local Bookstores.** Browse the subject category of your book in bookstores. See how your idea compares with similar books on the market. Tell bookstore owners or store managers you are publishing a book and would like their advice. You may want to call in advance to set up a convenient time to meet. After the meeting, send a thank-you note. When your book is released they may be more inclined to offer a book signing and carry your title. Online bookstores such as *Amazon.com* and *B&N.com* are also a good source to search for books in your subject category.

❏ **Public Libraries** have a wealth of free information. Visit the reference desk and become familiar with the following publications and any others they recommend for the self-publisher. Many libraries have free access to the Internet.

Literary Market Place
A valuable resource listing agents, associations, book clubs,
reviewers, news services, radio and TV stations.

Books in Print & Forthcoming Books
Lists all titles currently in print in the United States.
Also includes the authors' and publishers' names.

❏ **Read Books.** Benefit from other people's experiences by reading their books on self-publishing. I find the following publications to be worthwhile and refer to them often.

The Self-Publishing Manual	**Complete Guide to Self-Publishing**
By Dan Poynter	By Tom & Marilyn Ross

Two very comprehensive books on self-publishing, including what you need to know to write, print and sell your own book.

A Simple Guide to Marketing Your Book	**1001 Ways to Market Your Book**
By Mark Ortman	By John Kremer

Two handbooks for planning and promoting your marketing campaign with ideas, tips, references and suggestions on selling books.

❏ **OnLine Services & The Internet.** Connect electronically to people with similar interests. Various discussion groups *(newsgroups)* and research archives are accessible to anyone with a computer, and online service provider. By doing a search on words such as *self-publishing,* a subscriber can browse, research, meet or post a question to others who may be of help. Check your phone book for a local Internet Service Provider or contact any of the three national commercial providers listed below. For high speed Internet service, contact your local telephone company.

- America Online (800) 827-6364
- Microsoft Network (800) 373-3676
- SBC / Yahoo (800) 776-3449

Business Matters

All too often we forget that writing is an art and publishing is a business. For practical, tax and legal reasons it is important to establish a business structure in which your publishing venture can thrive.

❏ Think of a few **names** and **logos** with which to identify your publishing business. Avoid appearing too small by using your own name. Invent a name that is simple, easy to remember, descriptive and will not limit future publications. Once you have narrowed your choices, check the following resources in the library to avoid name duplication with another publisher.

- **Small Press Record of Books in Print**
- **Publishers Directory by Gale Research**
- **Books in Print (Publisher listing)**

Business is something which,
if you don't have any, you go out of.

❑ Plan a **budget** for publishing your book. Decisions between what you *want* and what you can *afford* will be easier with a budget. Expect to spend anywhere from $1000 to $50,000 depending on the type of book, the way the book is published, quantity printed and marketing plans. Three major areas of expense will be:

Book Preparation • **Printing** • **Promotion**

A general guideline for planning the promotional budget is to set aside $.50 to $1.00 per book printed.

❑ Apply for a **business license** with your state and local governments. Before you apply, decide on a type of business structure: *Sole Proprietorship*, *Partnership*, or *Corporation*. Most first time publishers choose *Sole Proprietorship* because it is the easiest to form. Talk to a banker, lawyer or the Small Business Administration for advice on starting a business.

Small Business Administration (SBA)
200 N College St # A2015
Charlotte NC 28202
(800) 827-5722 (Answer Desk)
www.sba.gov

❑ Protect your privacy and rent a **Box** from the Post Office for your mailing address. Request information on bulk mailing permits as well as postal rates. Postage will be a major expense, so know your options to manage mailing costs.

❑ Professionalize your business image with **stationery**. Print letterheads, envelopes, business cards and shipping labels with your name, address and logo. Project an image which will instill confidence in people who may want to do business with you. Single title author-publishers must overcome the stigma of being perceived as unprofessional.

Trade Registrations

❑ The *International Standard Book Number* **(ISBN)** is the ten digit number (soon to be 13) on the back of every book. The numbers identify the publisher and the book title. The book trade uses this number to order, price and keep track of inventory. Most wholesalers and bookstores are reluctant to stock a book that does not have this number clearly printed on the back cover. The numbers are available through R.R. Bowker. There is a handling fee of about $250 and you will receive 10 sets of ISBN numbers. They will arrive on a computer printout sheet reserved for your selection. The remaining nine set of numbers can be used for revised editions and future publications.

After you select a number from the computer printout sheet, activate by completing the **Advance Book Information (ABI)** form included with your ISBN order. By submitting an ABI form, your book will be listed in *Books in Print* at no charge. Call R.R. Bowker and request a publisher's information packet on how to apply for an ISBN number.

R.R. Bowker (ISBN Agency)
121 Chanlon Rd
New Providence NJ 07974
(888) 269-5372
www.isbn.org

❑ Set a **publication date** far enough in the future to give you time to print, submit for review, announce your book and generate advance sales. Your publication date is *not* the date your book comes back from the printer. The publication date is when you are releasing your book for sale to the public. The best publication date for the self-publisher is the first quarter of the year because this allows your copyright date to live a full year and still be new. The two major buying seasons for the publishing industry are Spring and Fall.

❑ **Copyright** protection lasts your life plus 70 years. This is done by using the copyright symbol with the year and your name (Copyright © 2003 by John Doe) and including it on the copyright page of your manuscript. Also, when your manuscript is complete, send yourself a *notarized* copy by *registered mail* and place unopened in storage. This is evidence of a specific date within the copyright year. Finally, when you get your books back from the printer, apply in writing with the copyright office in Washington, DC. Order in advance by phone the circulars on Copyright and form TX which is package #109. They are free of charge. Call (202) 707-3000 or visit their website: *www.copyright.gov*

❑ If you plan to make sales to the library market, apply for a **Library of Congress Card Catalog Number (LCCN)** and a publisher's **Catalog in Publication (CIP)**. These numbers will go on the copyright page of your book. There is no charge for the LCCN and a $150 charge for the CIP number. Request information from the following:

Preassigned LCCN Number	CIP number for single title publisher
Library of Congress Cataloging in Publication Division Washington DC 20540 (202) 707-9797 http://pcn.loc.gov/pcn	**Quality Books** 1003 W Pines Rd Oregon IL 61061 (815) 732-4450 www.quality-books.com

❑ **Barcodes** (Bookland EAN) are those vertical lines on the back of books. This enables a price scanner to identify the title, ISBN number and price. The cost is about $40. You will need the ISBN number **before** you can order one. Bookland EAN has become a requirement by most of the book trade.

Data Index, Inc. Box 1647 Snohomish WA 98292 (800) 426-2183 www.dataindex.com	**Fotel-GGX Associates, Inc.** 1125 E St Charles Rd #100 Lombard IL 60148 (800) 834-4920 www.fotel.com

Preparing the Manuscript

❏ If you use other people's words (not ideas) in your book, you must get **permission**. Send a request to the publisher by certified mail stating *what* you want to quote, *how* you will use it and *where* you will give credit. Normally you will get permission without cost. Copying and selling words of another author without written permission is called plagiarism and is illegal.

❏ **Editing.** A copy editor can clarify and strengthen what you want to say and how you say it. This includes clarity, consistency and the overall correctness of the manuscript. Contact a local newspaper or magazine to see if an editor or writer is willing to do it, or can recommend a colleague. Another option is to find an English teacher or graduate student from a local college who would love to receive acknowledgment in your book in exchange for assistance. Also, see the Yellow Pages for "Editorial Services" listing.

> In editing: review slowly, question everything
> and ask yourself, "Are the statements I am
> making true and verifiable?"

❏ Ask five eagle-eyed friends to **proofread** your manuscript for grammar, spelling, usage and punctuation. Do not rely on your computer's spell checker since it doesn't know whether you want to use "to" "too" or "two". It is quite common to rewrite your manuscript several times before it is ready to print . . . so be patient. Changes become costly after the manuscript goes to the printer. Include those people who help in the book's acknowledgments.

> Realize how editing and proofreading influence the
> quality of your book. Seek competent help in these
> areas to reduce post-printing regrets.

❏ **Typesetting & Layout.** This has to do with the selection and placement of your illustrations, graphs, pictures and text. In other words: how the inside of your book will look. The goal of the layout design is to communicate a consistent visual message throughout the book, making it easier to read and use. Browse books in bookstores and libraries to use as models for your own layout. A professional typesetter's fee can range from $4-10 per page. Thus, it may be cost-effective to purchase a computer, desktop software and a printer to do it yourself.

• **Page Layout Margins.** The layout margin is the space between the edge of the paper and where the text starts. That compensates for trimming during the printing process. Typically a .5 to 1.5 inch margin is adequate, depending on the design, size of book and type of binding you use. For example, this book uses a .625 inch margin.

• **Typeface & Font.** Most books use a Serif typeface for the *main body* of the text instead of sans serif type because it is easier to read and looks more professional. See the samples below. Handwritten copy or calligraphy may be suitable for certain publications, such as poetry or children's books. However, too much handwritten copy is hard to read and may detract from the flavor and intention of your book.

Serif   sans serif

• **Illustrations.** Illustrations can range from charts, photographs and artwork to anything that is not typeset. In planning the layout, leave enough space for the illustrations to later scan them in with a computer. Contact your book manufacturer or graphic designer for preferred format.

The Cover Design

The goal of the cover design is to *get people's attention.* Books are often sold on the merits of the cover alone; thus, the cover should capture the essence of your book. Whether displayed online or in a bookstore, your cover becomes the focal point. It is *well worth* the investment to hire a **graphic designer** with *book design* experience. Expect to pay $200 for a basis cover design to over $2,500 for an eye-catching design.

❑ People's first impressions come from the title of your book. Keep your **book title** brief, vivid and descriptive. As a rule of thumb, the title should be legible from 10 feet. The **subtitle** gives you an added sales message, describing your book in greater detail. Once you have narrowed possible book titles, search *Amazon.com,* and in the library: *Books in Print* and *Forthcoming Books* to avoid title duplication.

❑ If you think the book's **spine** is unimportant in the design, consider how many books in a bookstore are faced out that way. If space permits, include on the spine the title of the book, author's and publisher's names and logo.

❑ The **back cover** should convince the potential book buyers they are making the right decision by purchasing your book. Make it easy, interesting and informative for the browser to review. The back cover might include:

- Book's description and benefits to the reader
- Reviews, Endorsements and Testimonials
- Author's bio and picture
- ISBN, Bar Code, Price and Subject Category

❑ The easiest way to get **testimonials** or **endorsements** is to ask for them. Ask experts or celebrities in your field to review your manuscript and submit their impressions. Get permission in writing to print their comments in your book.

*Whenever I am asked what kind of
writing is the most lucrative,
I have to say: ransom notes!*

H.N. Swanson

2. Printing

Book Manufacturers

Get bids from a *Book Manufacturer* instead of a local printer. Book manufacturers have the equipment to print and bind books themselves, instead of sending out the work and marking up the price. If your book is more than 50 pages and you are printing more than 100 copies, chances are the prices will be much lower through a book manufacturer.

❑ Cheapest isn't always best. Consider **quality, service** and **support.** If a problem arises - and printing is fertile ground for problems - whose side will your printer be on, yours or his? Paying a little more for peace of mind is often worth it. Request samples and check references before you decide.

❑ Request **proofs** and a **cover matchprint** from your printer before your book goes to final press. This means you'll see and approve what the text and cover color will look like before it is printed. This is also the time to check for typographical errors or pages missing or out of sequence. There may be a charge for this service, but it is comforting to have the chance to make last minute changes.

❑ Most printers will print about 10% too many or too few books. These are called **over-** or **under-runs**. Ask what the over-runs will cost. They usually cost less, thus lowering the overall cost per copy of your book. Reprints are usually less expensive from the same printer because of reduced setup costs. Still, get other quotes to keep everyone honest.

❑ It's more economical to print in **even signatures.** This means the number of pages a printing press can print at one time. Most book manufacturers use a 16 or 32 page signature, depending on the size of the book (for example: 32 for 8.5x5.5 and 16 for 8.5x11). Divide the pages of your book by 16 or 32 and you will know how many signatures the printer will use. If your book is a page or two over an even signature, reduce the printing cost by editing them out.

❑ **Retail Price.** Search bookstores for comparable books to use as price models. A common mistake for self-publishers is to price their book either too high or too low. Printing costs do affect the retail price of the book. Don't expect your first printing to be very profitable, particularly when printing a small quantity. Reprints are far more profitable because of reduced setup costs, assuming you don't make too many changes to the book. Set a cover price that would allow for a profit giving a 55% discount for distribution.

Preparing a Printing Estimate

To prepare a price quote from a book manufacturer, you will need to know:

- Quantity
- Total page count
- Type of paper (text and cover)
- How many colors on the cover and cover coating
- Type of binding
- Size of the book
- Number of pictures (black and white or color)
- Packaging and shipping costs

❑ **Quantity.** How many books should you order? The more you print, the less each costs. Strike a balance between printing enough copies to keep your unit cost down and too many copies where you're stuck with a garage full of unsold books.

Typically, small publishers will order between 500 and 3500 books in the first printing. The only time to order more is if most are pre-sold. You can always re-order when your inventory gets low. Remember, reprints generally cost less barring many changes. Changes require new setup charges. Plan on 3 to 5 weeks for delivery.

❑ **Page Count.** To figure the total page count in your book, include the *front* and the *back* matter. The *front matter* is all the pages before the main text: Title Pages, Copyright Page, Acknowledgments, Preface, Foreword, Introduction, Table of Contents and Dedication. The *back matter* includes all pages in a book after the main text: Afterword, Appendix, Bibliography, Glossary and Index.

❑ **Paper.** Unless you are doing an art or full color specialty book, most printers will suggest a 50, 60, or 70 lb. white offset. 60 lb. paper is most common. The higher the weight, the heavier and more opaque the paper. The thickness (bulk) of the paper is measured by PPI (pages per inch). The lower the PPI, the bulkier the paper, thus the thicker the book. Ask the printer for this number to determine the width of the book's spine. Divide book's page count by PPI to get spine width.

> One of your greatest expenses will be postage and shipping.
> The paper you select will influence this expense.
> Heavier paper costs more to ship.

❑ **Cover Paper.** Will the book be softcover or hardcover? Because of lower production costs, most books are now softcover. The standard paper for softcover is a 10 or 12 point C1S (coated one side) cover stock. Hardcover books will use a dust jacket, and 80 or 100 lb enamel paper is most common. Order five to ten percent extra book covers or dust jackets, as they are useful for various promotional purposes.

❏ **Cover Coating.** This is what protects the book cover and enhances the color. There are various kinds available: Lay flat plastic film lamination, matted, aqueous coating or UV. Ask the printers what type they use and the advantages of each. Request samples. This book uses film lamination.

❏ **Binding.** This is what holds the book together. Common types are: Perfect Bound (softcover), Otabind (softcover that lies open), Case Bound (hardcover), Spiral or Saddle Stitched (stapled). How the book will be used will influence the type of binding. This book is Perfect Bound.

> Bookstores frown upon Spiral and Saddle Stitched books because you can't read them when faced spine out on the shelf.

❏ **Book Size.** The conventional and common 5.5 x 8.5 is suitable for both hard and softcover, and is one of the most economical to print. Other standard sizes include 6 x 9 and 8.5 x 11. The further you get away from the standard, the more expensive the book is to produce.

❏ **Pictures.** Color photos can be beautiful, although expensive because of color separation and extra print run fees. When appropriate, B&W photos are more affordable. With a digital camera or scanner, images can be shot or scanned and imported onto your manuscript. Consult your graphic designer and book manufacturer for required file format, whether TIF or JPG, and the number of DPI (dots per inch) for photos. 72 to 300 DPI is typical depending if color or B&W.

❏ **Packaging.** Ask your printer the most economical way to ship your books. Plan for storage by asking the printer the size and weight of the cartons. A packaging option to consider is shrink wrapping. This is a clear plastic wrap used to protect the books and should be considered if you intend to store your books in a garage or unheated area.

List of Book Manufacturers

These printers specialize in the manufacturing of books. Get all estimates **in writing** before you make a decision. Most book manufactures prefer your finished layout (and cover) sent to them in digital format. PDF *(Adobe Acrobat's Portable Document Format file)* or from a popular desktop publishing program is most common. Extra charges add-up when paying book manufacturers to convert your manuscript into a preferred format. Printing estimates are also available online.

Bang Printing
1473 Highway 18 E
Brainerd MN 56401
(218) 829-2877
www.bangprinting.com

McNaughton & Gunn
960 Woodland Dr
Saline MI 48176
(734) 429-5411
www.bookprinters.com

Edwards Brothers
2500 S State St
Ann Arbor MI 48106
(734) 769-1000
www.edwardsbrothers.com

Sheridan Books
613 E Industrial Dr
Chelsea MI 48118
(800) 475-9145
www.sheridanbooks.com

Central Plains
22234 "C" St
Winfield KS 67156
(877) 278-2726
www.centralplainsbook.com

Thomson-Shore
7300 W Joy Rd
Dexter MI 48130
(734) 426-3939
www.tshore.com

Malloy, Inc
5411 Jackson Rd
Ann Arbor MI 48103
(800) 722-3231
www.malloy.com

United Graphics
2916 Marshall Ave
Mattoon IL 61938
(217) 235-7161
www.unitedgraphicsinc.com

Print Quantity Needed (PQN) Printers *(Short runs from 100 to 1000 copies)*

BookMasters
2541 Ashland Rd
Mansfield OH 44905
(419) 589-5100
www.bookmasters.com

Gorham Printing
334 Harris Rd
Rochester WA 98579
(800) 837-0970
www.gorhamprinting.com

Digital Demand Publishing

Digital technology is quickly changing the way books are produced, published and distributed. **Online publishing** has become an attractive alternative to the high costs of conventional publishing, making it easier for writers to become published authors. The two general ways are:

• **Electronic Books.** This is when you submit your manuscript in a digital word processing format, then your manuscript is converted into a document people can purchase over the Internet. Electronic books are sometimes called eBooks, virtual books, digital books or online books. eBooks are paperless. They are a full-length manuscript which is downloaded as a data file directly to the purchaser's computer. The self-publisher retains *all* rights and is free to print through conventional means if the demand warrants. The cost to produce an eBook is considerably less than conventional means. Fees typically run under $600.

eBook publishing is a prudent way to test market your book or publish when there is a specialized or limited audience. Since there is no inventory, an eBook is sold for significantly less than a traditional hard or softcover copy. Orders are handled through a contracted eBook distributor, then a royalty is paid to you for each sale. Royalties range from 30% to 50%. Even though your eBook will be made available through many online bookstores, it is still the responsibility of the self-publisher to actively promote their eBook.

• **Print-on-Demand (POD).** Most eBook distributors can also print your book in a hard or softcover version. Print-on-Demand means your book is printed and shipped to the quantity ordered. If a bookstore wants to purchase a single copy of your book, it is able to order without the transaction going through you. This eliminates the self-publisher's cost of inventory, shipping and returns. If the demand for your book becomes substantial, then printing through conventional means may be justified.

Certain constraints do exist with POD technology. Books that are more than one hundred pages and with few photographs print best. Although the photo reproduction technology is improving, pictures lack the crispness of lithography. POD books carry a slightly higher retail price to compensate for production, convenience, wholesale discounts and a profit. Many eBook distributors have contracted with Ingram Book Company making your book available to any bookstore nationwide, and *Amazon.com* for online purchases.

The following companies specialize in the production and distribution of eBooks and POD books. See *Literary Market Place* in the library for additional listings.

1st Books Library
1663 Liberty Dr
Bloomington IN 47403
(800) 839-8640
www.1stbooks.com

Trafford Publishing
Suite 6E - 2333 Government St
Victoria, BC V8T 4P4
(888) 232-4444
www.trafford.com

Universal Publishing
7525 NW 61 Terrace #2603
Parkland FL 33067
(800) 636-8329
www.upublish.com

Xlibris Publishing
436 Walnut St 11th Fl
Philadelphia PA 19106
(888) 759-4274
www.xlibris.com

POD technology is the future of book printing. As this technology matures, bookstores will be able to produce hard or softcover editions of *any* book in digital format with electronic kiosks. The customer can view a portion, or the entire book, read reviews and order right on the spot with a credit or debit card. Depending on your book's purpose, marketing plan and demand, it still may be more advantageous to print, inventory, distribute and promote through traditional means.

*Publishing is a very mysterious business.
It is hard to predict what kind of sale
or reception a book will have.*

Thomas Wolfe

3. Announcing Your Book

Letting the Industry Know

❑ Let the book trade know that you have published a book. Orders can come most unexpectedly by having your title listed in several directories. Most of these listings are free. Write or phone to request an application.

International Standard Book Numbering Agency (ISBN)
When you submit your **ABI** (Advanced Book Information)
form with your publication date and ISBN number, you
will automatically be listed in *Books in Print*.

Library of Congress Catalog Card Number.
When you request an LC number, your book will be listed in a
catalog enabling libraries to locate your book more easily.

Cumulative Book Index & Vertical File Index
H.W. Wilson Co
950 University Ave
Bronx NY 10452
(718) 588-8400
www.hwwilson.com

**Small Press Record of Books in Print &
International Directory of Little Magazines and Small Presses.**
Dustbooks
Box 100
Paradise CA 95967
(530) 877-6110
www.dustbooks.com

ABA Book Buyers Handbook
American Booksellers Assn
828 S Broadway
Tarrytown NY 10591
(800) 637-0037
www.bookweb.org

Gale Directories
Publishers Directory
27500 Drake Rd
Farmington Hills MI 48331
(800) 347-4253
www.galegroup.com

Pre-Publication Reviews

Besides yourself, who will think your book is great? Pre-publication reviews are directed at the trade (libraries, wholesalers and bookstores) **before** the publication date and the release of your book. This helps the trade evaluate new titles, and influences its purchasing decisions.

❏ **Trade Reviews.** To be reviewed, at least **90** days *before* the publication date, the major trade review magazines want to see: a galley (NOT a finished book), sample cover (if available), a fact sheet (describing the features of the book such as title, subtitle, description, page count, ISBN and LC numbers, binding, price and wholesale availability), author's bio, any endorsements from respected authorities and publicity plans. Write a *brief* cover letter stating *what* the book is about, *why* you wrote it and *how* it is unique from others on the market. Send all this by first class mail. This is no guarantee your book will be reviewed. However, even one favorable review could generate substantial advance sales. In addition, any reviews you receive can be used on your promotional literature and printed on the back cover of reprinted books. It is worth a phone call to inquire about the full name (with correct spelling) of the person to whom you will submit a review package. Also, inquire about any special submission guidelines. Follow up all submissions with a finished book. See *Literary Market Place* for additional review sources.

Booklist /American Library Assn	**Bloomsbury Review**
50 E Huron St	1553 Platte St #206
Chicago IL 60611	Denver CO 80202
(312) 944-6780	(303) 455-3123
www.ala.org	www.bookforum.com /bloomsbury
Chicago Tribune Books	**Library Talk**
435 N Michigan Ave	480 E Wilson Bridge Rd #L
Chicago Il 60611	Worthington OH 43085
(312) 222-3232	(614) 436-7107
www.chicagotribune.com	www.linworth.com

ForeWord Magazine	L.A. Times Book Review
129-1/2 E Front St	Times Mirror Square
Traverse City MI 49684	Los Angeles CA 90053
(231) 933-3699	(213) 237-5000
www.forewordmagazine.com	www.latimes.com
Library Journal	N.Y. Review of Books
360 Park Ave S	1755 Broadway
New York NY 10010	New York NY 10019
(646) 746-6819	(212) 757-8070
www.libraryjournal.com	www.nybooks.com
N.Y. Times Book Review	Publishers Weekly
229 W 43rd St	245 W 17th St
New York NY 10036	New York NY 10011
(212) 556-1234	(212) 463-6758
www.nytimes.com	www.publishersweekly.com
San Francisco Chronicle Book Review	School Library Journal
901 Mission St	360 Park Ave S
San Francisco CA 94103	New York NY 10010
(415) 777-7042	(646) 746-6819
www.sfgate.com	www.slj.com

• **Galleys.** A galley is not a finished book, but a representation of the finished book. Instead of paying to have galley proofs professionally printed and bound, consider using photo-copies of your camera-ready manuscript.

❏ **A News Release.** A news release is a one page (double spaced) write-up about your book. Your release should reflect the personality of your book by building around one central theme. Write in the inverted pyramid style, with the most important information at the top, followed by more specific details. Make the release sound like news and avoid "hype". Get to the point quickly. A news release is not advertising copy; it is designed to report information. Keep to the facts, leaving out flowery adjectives, superlatives and opinion. Answer throughout the release, the *Who, What, When, Where* and *Why* (or How) about the book. With so many books vying for publicity, what is it about your book that gives it news value (information which excites the reviewer)?

Post-Publication Reviews

Post-publication reviews are intended to reach the purchaser of your book. It is very expensive and inefficient to send review copies to every book reviewer. Target those from whom you have the best chance of getting a review.

• **Giving Review Copies Away.** Giving books away can become an expensive proposition, particularly when you include the cost of postage. A simple rule is to budget *at least* 5% of the books from your first printing as review copies and give them to the people who can *do you the most good.* Despite the expense, giving away review copies can be an extremely good promotional investment. Stamp REVIEW COPY, NOT FOR SALE on any copy you give away to discourage people from selling or returning that book to a wholesaler for a refund. Keep good records of giveaways as they are a tax-deductible business expense.

❏ **Newspapers.** Most newspaper book reviewers receive more solicitations each week than they can review each month. Review space is at a premium. Nevertheless, any mention of your book will help sales. *If* your book has a wide general appeal, mail a news release and book request post-card *(or book)* to the major daily newspapers, targeting the appropriate editor (Food, Features, Business, etc). Rent a mailing list from one of the mailing list sources on page 54. Local newspapers and magazines are your best bets to get a book review or a news article. Because you are local news, they may be inclined to give you preference over others.

❏ **Experts in the Field.** Send a review copy to authorities or experts on the subject of your book, asking for their endorse-ments. This is a wonderful way to get influential people talking about your book. See *Contemporary Authors* at the library for their names and mailing addresses.

❏ **Magazine Reviews.** Target magazines where subscribers' interests match the subject of your book. Find out what magazines *they* read and send a copy of your book and a press release to those magazines' book review editors. See the *Standard Periodical Directory* in the public library for listings of specialty magazines.

❏ **Newsletter Reviews.** The number of newsletters has boomed during the past decade, now accounting for nearly one-third of all publications. This has resulted in more opportunities to get your book mentioned or reviewed. In addition, most associations publish a newsletter which is mailed to their members and often has a book review section. See the *Oxbridge Directory of Newsletters* and *Encyclopedia of Associations* in the library.

❏ **Free-Lance Reviewers.** If your book is of general interest, rent a mailing list of free-lance book reviewers around the country (see page 54 for mailing lists brokers). Send a news release, fact sheet, and a book request return postcard *(or book)* immediately upon the book's release.

Book Review Tips

Choose only those reviewers most suitable to the subject of your book.

Follow up immediately with anyone who requests a review copy of your book.

Don't be surprised if you don't get an overwhelming response from reviewers.

The critic is the only independent source of information. The rest is advertising.
Pauline Kael

Literature is like any other trade;
you will never sell anything unless
you go to the right shop.

George Bernard Shaw

4. Distribution

How are people going to find your book if they decide to buy it? Reviews, publicity and advertising are worthless unless your book is readily available to the reader. At least 2-6 months before the release date, decide on how you will distribute your book, whether through conventional, alternative or a combination of both channels of distribution. It is in the self-publisher's interest to use a variety of distribution channels.

❏ **Consignments.** This is a standard inventory stocking practice in the publishing industry, especially in the conventional channels of distribution. What this means is you don't get paid until after your book has been sold and shipped from their warehouse. Not until then are you paid (usually 90-120 days later to allow time to deduct for any returns). All unsold books are returned to you when the demand ceases. A 15-25% return rate is common, so the lack of promotion will only increase the return rate.

❏ **Promotional Plan.** Most channels of distribution want to know how *you* are going to create a demand for your book if they stock it. That's right: the self-publisher is responsible for creating the demand. Before you approach the conventional channels of distribution, have a step-by-step promotional plan (See page 43) for your book which answers:

- **WHO** is your target audience?

- **WHERE** are they to be found?

- **WHAT** will be done to create a demand?

Conventional Channels of Distribution

❑ **Bookstores.** These are considered the traditional "brick & mortar" stores. There are many kinds: General, College, Used and Religious to list just a few. Independently owned bookstores make up a shrinking half *(because of the growth of online and chain stores)* of all the bookstores in the USA. Bookstores purchase a majority of their books through wholesalers or distributors. Most bookstores prefer buying books through a wholesaler or distributor because they carry numerous titles, simplifying their ordering procedure. Bookstores typically purchase at a 40% discount off the list price. *The American Book Trade Directory* has listings.

❑ **Chain Bookstores.** Barnes & Noble and Borders Books & Music are the largest. Their inventories are tightly controlled with short shelf life for slow-moving books. Recognize the risk of selling to the chains. They may order your entire stock and pay you 90 days later, leaving you to finance the next printing. Then, all of a sudden, they return the unsold books asking for a refund. A more prudent approach would be to coordinate purchases and promotional effort with local or regional chain buyers. This way the sales of one area finance the expansion into another.

Barnes & Noble	Borders Books & Music
122 Fifth Ave	100 Phoenix Dr
New York NY 10011	Ann Arbor MI 48108
(212) 633-3377	(734) 477-1100
www.barnesandnoble.com	www.borders.com

❑ **Book Wholesalers.** Wholesalers stock, pick, pack, ship and collect, then pay you 90 days later on orders received for your book. For this service, they want a 55% discount off the list price. Most are *"Demand Wholesalers"* meaning they fulfill orders for your book based on the demand that *you* create. There are many wholesalers in the country, some national, some regional and many specializing in niches.

Is your book of primarily local or regional interest? Ask local booksellers which regional wholesaler they order through. Contact that wholesaler, share your promotional plans, and establish a vendor account.

Ingram Book Company and **Baker & Taylor Books** are the nation's largest national book wholesalers with branches throughout the United States. Ask about a vendor account.

Baker & Taylor Books	**Ingram Book Company**
1120 US Route 22 E	One Ingram Blvd
Bridgewater NJ 08807	LaVergne TN 37086
(908) 218-3803	(615) 793-5000
www.btol.com	www.ingrambook.com

Both Baker & Taylor and Ingram offer ebook and print-on-demand distribution services. This means they are able to print books one-at-a-time based on the demand for your title, relieving you of the cost of inventory and distribution.

Replica Books (Baker & Taylor)	**Lightning Source (Ingram Books)**
(908) 541-7391	(615) 213-5815
www.btol.com	www.lightningsource.com

❑ **Book Distributors.** Distributors differ from wholesalers in that they sell your book through commissioned sales reps and a catalog. Depending on the type of distributor, they will introduce your title to wholesalers and bookstores, thus freeing you to concentrate on promotion. They buy at a 55% to 67% discount off the list price *(plus inbound shipping)*. Some may require an exclusive arrangement. Before signing an exclusive agreement, clarify **what** is meant by "exclusive". Do not limit your book to an exclusive arrangement, preventing you from selling to markets which the distributor doesn't sell to. Contact distributors 2-6 months before your book is released to allow them enough time to go through their selection process. See the *Literary Market Place* or *A Simple Guide to Marketing Your Book* for additional listings. The following are common types of distributors:

• **Specialty Distributors.** When your book is targeted toward a specific market niche or subject area *(Outdoor, Health, Ethnic etc.)*, specialty distributors can help you reach that reader. Their discounts vary between 55% - 65% off list.

• **Mass Market Distributors.** If your book fits their format, they will place your title in non-bookstore locations such as supermarkets, airports, and newsstands. Their fee is 55% off list. *Require* all returns in resalable condition. Mass Market distributors traditionally have a high return rate and a short shelf life. If a book doesn't sell *fast,* it is replaced.

• **Library Distributors.** They specialize in selling books to libraries. Contact the two distributors listed below and ask for a vendor application. Both work on consignment and require a 55% discount.

Quality Books
1003 W Pines Rd
Oregon IL 61061
(815) 732-4450
www.quality-books.com

Unique Books
5010 Kemper Ave
St Louis MO 63139
(314) 776-6695
www.uniquebooksinc.com

• **Master Distributors.** If your book is of general interest and you plan to promote your title nationally, consider a master distributor to carry your book. A master distributor will get your book into the major regional and national book wholesalers and perhaps present your title to major independent and chain bookstores. A master distributor will coordinate your promotional efforts with his national sales rep network. They want a 63-67% discount off the list price, and may add monthly fees. Below are four master distributors to request information about their title acquisition procedure. Most will want an exclusive right to sell to the book trade (bookstores and libraries). That leaves you to sell through alternative channels. Most master distributors prefer publishers with more than one title.

Have a *detailed* promotional plan before approaching.

BookWorld Services 1933 Whitfield Park Loop Sarasota FL 34243 (941) 758-8094 www.bookworld.com	**Independent Publishers Group** 814 N Franklin St Chicago IL 60610 (312) 337-0747 www.ipgbook.com
National Book Network (Biblio) 4720 Boston Way Lanham MD 20706 (301) 459-3366 www.nbnbooks.com	**Publishers Group West** 1700 4th St Berkeley CA 94710 (510) 528-1444 www.pgw.com

Alternative Channels of Distribution

If your book *does not* have a broad, general appeal for conventional channels of distribution, all is not lost. Most books sold in the United States are sold through alternative channels. Books on a specific subject or tight market niche may find alternative channels the easiest to secure and most profitable. Consult the *Literary Market Place* for additional listings of alternative channels of distribution.

❑ **Book Clubs.** Book clubs may be interested in purchasing book club rights or actual copies of your book when printed. While some special interest book clubs will buy books regardless of the publication date, most prefer 6 months notice before the publication date.

❑ **Catalog Houses.** Have you ever received a catalog in the mail that featured books? Thousands of companies in the United States send out catalogs annually, many including books. Send a copy of your book to mail order catalog companies that specialize in the subject area of your title. For mail order catalogs that feature books, see *The Directory of Mail Order Catalogs* and *Literary Market Place* at the public library. Visit *www.buyersindex.com* on the Internet for a listing of more than 5000 catalog companies by specialty.

❑ **Gift Stores.** Over 30% of the population have never been in a bookstore. Having your book displayed in retail outlets such as gift and card shops is a way to reach some of those people. Unlike bookstores, the gift market does not return books. However, the discount is a little higher, generally 50% off list. Most gift stores prefer buying through gift reps. Many large cities have wholesale gift-center showrooms where manufacturers and gift rep organizations display their wares for wholesale purchase. Check phone book for listings.

❑ **Specialty Retail Outlets.** Not everyone buys books in bookstores. Home improvement centers, drugstores, auto supply dealers, kitchen shops and health food stores are all prospects if your book fits their market. In other words, approach people or companies who can tie your book into the marketing of their own products. Most of these sales are made on a non-returnable basis at a negotiated discount, typically 40-50%.

❑ **Direct Sales.** Any sales made by-passing a middle man are your most profitable. You keep 100% of the retail price less any expenses and given discounts. When selling by mail, include a shipping and handling charge.

❑ **Fulfillment Services.** These companies offer warehous-ing and order-processing services (toll-free number & credit card purchases over the phone) for your book. Most want a percentage and/or a monthly fee for their service. As you promote your title, make reference to the service's toll-free number for ordering 24 hours a day. Contact the following:

BookMasters	**Publication Services**
2541 Ashland Rd	8803 Tara Ln
Mansfield OH 44905	Austin TX 78737
(419) 589-5100	(800)460-0500
www.bookmasters.com	www.psifulfillment.com

❏ **Online Bookstores.** These are businesses that have a Web Site on the Internet and will list your book in their online bookstore. People around the world can browse a book's contents, read excerpts, and get ordering information from their computer. Unless you are publishing through a print-on-demand distributor (page 26), do a search on *google.com* for special interest bookstores that are on the Web that may closely match your book's market niche. Amazon.com's Advantage Program is a convenient way for self-publisher's to have their book listed and sold at their site. Each of the "big three" have their own vendor of record program.

Amazon.com
www.amazon.com/advantage

Barnes & Noble
www.bn.com/help/b_faq.asp

Borders Books & Music
www.borders.com

❏ **Subsidiary Rights.** This is when you sell the rights of all or a portion of your book to someone else who will package it in a different form for his market. Some examples include: movie/TV rights, an excerpt for a magazine article, paperback or hardcover rights, electronic rights and foreign rights. Consider hiring an agent or attorney familiar with the right you are selling. See *Literary Market Place* in the library.

❏ **Remainder Dealers.** Remainder dealers help liquidate overstocks and remaining copies of your out-of-print books. They will purchase unsold books at pennies on the dollar. When all sales sources are exhausted, contact several remainder dealers to see who will give you the best price and terms. See *Literary Market Place* in the library.

❏ **Donations.** Another way to liquidate unsold books is to donate remaining and damaged books to a worthy cause or non-profit groups and take the tax write-off.

*The writing of a best-seller represents
only a fraction of the total effort
required to create one.*

Ted Nicholas

5. Creating a Demand

Developing a Promotional Plan

Promoting a book is generally the most important and demanding function for a self-publisher. There are more than 3000 new titles released each week, more than two million books in print, and the average bookstore stocks less than 50,000 titles. This contributes to a very crowded and competitive arena. The book trade has just one question: *"Will your book sell?"*

A book is a product, and like any other product it requires publicity and promotion. Potential readers must be made *aware* of your book, *how* it differs from similar books on the market and *where* they can purchase it. Proper planning is essential to give your book the best chance of success.

❏ **A Promotional Plan.** This answers the questions: *Who* is your target audience? *Where* are they found? *What* will be done to create a demand? Refer to page 9.

    • **WHO** is your audience and **WHERE** are they found? Typically, there are multiple audiences for your book. A technique to help you figure out *Who will buy your book* is to spend time in the library compiling lists of organizations, associations, corporations, hobbyists, occupations, experts and anyone else who will find value in knowing about your book. List those you want to reach first, second, third, etc. Review the list and see if there is any overlap. This will help you direct your efforts more efficiently and give you insight into the best ways to reach them.

The self-publisher actually has **two** categories of customers: *The Trade* and *The Reader*. The Trade consists of bookstores, wholesalers and libraries. The Reader is your target audience or end user. Research and promotional efforts must be allocated to both, particularly when pursuing conventional channels of distribution. (See page 35 on Distribution.)

When is the Trade and the Reader in the most favorable buying mood? Does your book have a seasonal twist? Publishers introduce new releases throughout the year with an emphasis on two seasons: Spring and Fall. The industry's largest trade show, Book Expo America *(www.reedexpo.com)*, occurs annually around the end of May. This is a key time for publishers to show their new titles to the Trade. Readers purchase books throughout the year with an emphasis on the holiday and gift seasons. The nature of your book is also a consideration as the timing may be built into your product and those you intend to reach.

  • **WHAT** will be done to create a demand? How will you let the reader know about your book and where to purchase copies? There are six general ways to reach the Reader through your promotions: *Mail, Fax, Phone, Online, The Media* and *In Person,* each having its cost advantages and disadvantages. People today are more accessible, yet harder to sell, stressing the importance of a tightly targeted and strong sales message. The remaining chapter will outline what you will need to promote your book, and the numerous ways to create a demand. With so many options, self-publishers have the luxury of time to systematically test several promotional options to find what works best. What works for one book may not work for another, thus the importance of proper planning. In the end, tracking sales will clearly define to *whom* and *where* your book will sell. Thus, you can adjust your promotional strategy accordingly.

Promotional Kit

There is no limit to what you can spend on promotional materials. It becomes a question of budget and what is practical. The following are suggestions for a basic promotional kit for the budget minded self-publisher.

• **News Release.** A one page (double-spaced) news release answers *why* you wrote the book, concentrating on what issue, solution or benefit your book will address for the Reader. This is what is mailed to announce the release of your book to reviewers, bookstores and the media. Keep it simple, factual, informative and interesting. See page 31.

• **Extra Book Covers.** Extra book covers come in handy as mailers or point of purchase display and can be used as part of your media kit. Many distributors will request extra covers for their sales force to use to sell your title.

• **Media Kit.** A Media Kit (often termed Press Kit) simply provides more information about you and your book. This gives an editor, producer, reporter or interviewer useful information for a book review, interview or article. In a glossy 8x11 pocket folder, include: a book, news release, author bio, photo, fact sheet, any reviews, news articles, endorsements and sample interview questions. The key is for the information to be well organized and easy to read as most interviewers *will not* read your book.

• **Fact Sheet.** A fact sheet outlines the basic features or facts of your book. On one page, include: title, subtitle, author, brief book description, ISBN/LC number, publication date, book size, page count, type of binding, weight, number of books per case and wholesale availability. The fact sheet answers important questions for reviewers, the media, editors, vendors and the book trade.

• **Photos.** Most interviewers want to know what you look like. Print 5x7 black & white promotional glossies of yourself that complement the message of your book. Pictures are often requested by reviewers, magazines, newspapers and even bookstores to promote your signing. Hire a professional photographer to snap the right pose. Today's digital cameras and jet ink printers offer a convenient way to produce your own glossies.

> Label all photos with a sticker on the back with book title, author's name and phone number. This will help avoid misplacement.

• **Reviews, Endorsements & Letters.** Save any reviews, endorsements, testimonials, fan mail and articles written about you or your book. These provide great sales copy for your promotional literature.

• **Book Request Postcard.** Print book request return postcards and include one with your news release when you are *not* sending a review copy of your book. Those interested in your news release message will respond, thus saving you the expense of mailing books randomly to uninterested people.

• **Brochure, Flyer or Postcard.** A full-color flyer is useful, catchy and professional. A helpful hint is to leave some blank space on the front or the back side to photocopy a specific promotional message at a future date. This enables you to adjust your flyer's message and use for many promotional situations. A 4x6 color post card with your book cover printed on one side and a sales message on the other can save on postage and envelope costs. Shop around, as prices vary from printer to printer.

Make it easy for people to do the things you request.

Ways to Create a Demand

Promotion and publicity are essential to your book's success. However, no one can predict the commercial success of a book. You can only give your book the best possible chance to succeed with the least amount of risk; then wait for the market to send its verdict. This section will outline the many ways you can create a demand for your book. See *A Simple Guide to Marketing Your Book* and *1001 Ways to Market Your Book* and for a more detailed collection of ideas.

❏ **Author's Tours.** Do you like to travel? Does your book have a broad appeal? If so, author's tours can be a rewarding, although expensive endurance test, but one of the best ways to reach a large book buying public. Pick the destination(s), and at least 6 weeks in advance, book yourself on as many TV and radio shows as possible. Inform all bookstores (in each area) of your promotional activity, encouraging them to have your book in stock. Select the area's most popular bookstore in which to do a lecture or reading and booksigning. Send notices to local newspapers outlining your activity, as they may be interested in an interview or at least a mention in their paper. Always bring extra books so you won't run out.

❏ **Book Signings**. Unless your signing is backed by a great deal of media promotion, it is doubtful that people will be lined up waiting for your autograph. However, a signing serves many purposes. Your book will be displayed in the store. You begin building a relationship with the store owner, manager and staff (who can recommend your title to their customers) and you leave behind signed copies which increases the book's appeal. Most bookstores are receptive to signings, as your presence will help pull customers into their store, resulting in free publicity for both you and them. Send the local media advance notice of your signing as most will list this free of charge.

❏ **Book Signing Party.** Kick off the release of your book with a book signing party at your home, office or local bookstore. Gather friends, family, neighbors, associates, colleagues and anyone else who would support you and your book's message. Invite the local media.

❏ **Seminars.** If you enjoy teaching - speaking, find a group, business, college or organization to sponsor and promote your seminar. This will help offset any costs incurred and provide a built-in endorsement for you and your book.

❏ **Readings & Lectures**. Local social, civic and business organizations are all looking for speakers. Use your expertise to promote your book. Most groups will let you sell directly to members after the presentation.

❏ **More on Libraries.** There are more than 100,000 libraries in the United States, ranging from academic to public, and they buy a lot of books. Your title becomes a permanent advertisement when sitting on their shelves. Many public libraries have an events coordinator or "Friends of the Library" groups who organize author and fundraising activities. Look to local libraries for generating publicity and reviews through signings, workshops and lectures. Libraries typically purchase books through wholesalers, and occasionally direct from the publisher.

❏ **Write Articles.** Since you know more about your topic than most people, share your knowledge and publicize your book at the same time. Many magazines, journals, newspapers and newsletters welcome newsworthy articles.

❏ **Fundraisers.** Most groups, schools and organizations are looking for ways to generate revenues. If there is a good fit, donate a percentage of your book sales to their cause in exchange for selling and endorsing your book.

❑ **Premiums & Incentives.** Many businesses offer premiums as incentives to their employees and customers. Why shouldn't that premium be your book? See the *Thomas Register* or their *Regional* directory in the library for a list of companies and products to find a tie-in.

❑ **Book Trade Shows**. The primary purpose of a regional or national book trade show is to introduce new titles to the trade. You may display your new book on your own, or pay someone else to do so. Bookstore owners who attend will browse and make seasonal buying decisions; this is an ideal opportunity to win shelf space in their stores.

❑ **Trade Shows & Conventions.** Selling your book at a trade show or convention can be a profitable experience. Assembled in one place is a high concentration of potential buyers. This becomes a great place to make valuable contacts and get exposure to an industry. Use the *Encyclopedia of Associations* in the library to find out what groups are holding meetings or conventions in your vicinity. The *Chamber of Commerce* and a city's *Convention Centers* are also helpful contacts.

❑ **Book, Art & Street Fairs.** Sponsors promote to the general public or to a niche group of people and thus are a great forum for showing and selling your book direct. Calculate your break-even point before paying for space. Sharing space with another author will reduce your costs.

❑ **Book Awards & Contests.** An award or a nomination can be a profitable and satisfying experience, generating free publicity for your book. Submit your title to the various organizations that offer such contests. See the *Literary Market Place* or *Writer's Market* in the library for listings.

The oldest books are still only just out
to those who have not read them.

❏ **The Media.** Print and electronic media (newspapers, magazines, radio and television) are under pressure to fill space or time with news. Media exposure gives an author expert status that even the largest advertising budget can't touch. The media needs you as much as you need them. For example, unsolicited news releases occupy nearly 20% of editorial space. Locally, you and your book are news and should have an edge to get air time or print space. See *The Directory of Publications and Broadcast Media* in the library. The following sell ways to reach the national media:

Radio-TV Interview Report	Talk Show Selects
Bradley Communications	Broadcast Interview Source
135 E Plumstead Ave	2233 Wisconsin Ave NW #301
Lansdowne PA 19050	Washington DC 20007
(800) 989-1400	(800) 932-7266
www.rtir.com	www.yearbook.com

• **Radio.** Radio is your most accessible form of publicity. If you enjoy talking about your book, you will enjoy radio interviews. More than 750 radio talk shows in the country are looking for interesting guests. Most conduct interviews over the phone, which means you don't have to leave your home. Some will even tape an interview to be aired at a future date. Phone the Program Director or Producer of the station and say: *"I have a story that will be of interest to your audience"*. Be prepared to quickly explain why your message will be important to their listeners. Make an interview with you sound appealing. Start off by interviewing on smaller stations to practice your message for the larger ones. The more stations you contact, the more interviews you will get. Assume the interviewer has not read your book. This is the case more often than not, and he will rely on the Media Kit you send him in advance. Phone bookstores in the stations broadcast area before your radio interview to ensure they have your book in stock. See *The American Book Trade Directory* in the library for national bookstore listings.

• **Newspapers.** Perhaps your book can address a lifestyle, business, gardening, travel or cooking issue. Send a news release and cover letter to the appropriate editor, with a possible story angle. If your book relates to a problem that just hit the headlines, get on the phone and try to secure an interview. More than 900 daily and weekly newspapers throughout the country are searching for news.

• **Television.** Wouldn't it be ideal if the major national talk show hosts invited you to discuss your book on their shows? When getting started, it is more realistic to be a guest on a local afternoon news program or a TV magazine talk show. Contact the show's producer with your story, convincing him of a possible angle for the show. Local cable access stations offer a great place to practice live interviews. TV leaves a powerful impression in the viewer's mind and can translate into an explosion of book sales.

• **Magazines.** Thousands of magazines cater to every audience you can imagine. Offer reprints of a portion of your book in exchange for a free ad and/or a byline at the end of your article. Include local and regional publications as they may be more accommodating to local authors. See *Standard Periodical Directory* at the public library for a compete listing of national magazines and their focus.

❏ **Word-of-Mouth.** Word-of-mouth can be the fastest and most efficient form of free advertising, especially now with the Internet. This happens when people have heard, seen, bought or read your book and told others about it. The more books in people's hands, the better the chance they will spread the word. Anything you can do to get people talking about your book will generate interest and sales. Media appearances and favorable reviews all contribute to word-of-mouth advertising.

❏ **Advertising.** After you have exhausted all other means of publicity, turn to paid advertising. Advertising comes in many forms, although the intent is always the same: to motivate a desired response. This is done by developing an ad that gains the readers' favorable attention, holds it long enough to get the intended message across and then motivates a predetermined action. When designing an ad, talk about the readers' interest, as they are interested in what the book will do for them. Two general rules of advertising success are **timing** and **repetition.**

• **Space Advertising.** Space advertising involves placing an advertisement or insert in newspapers, catalogs newsletters, books, magazines, or any supplement which targets your audience. Orders are placed by the customer by mail or calling a toll-free number, and then shipped by you or your fulfillment service. At the reference desk in the public library see:

Standard Rate and Data
Lists magazines, periodicals, demographics and their advertising rates.

Standard Periodical Directory
Directory of national magazines.

Directory of Publications & Broadcast Media
List daily and weekly newspapers in the United States.

• **Classified Ads.** This is one of the least expensive forms of advertising. Classified ads are best used to compile a good mailing list or to test market the pull of an ad instead of selling books. Offer free information in return for a self-addressed, stamped envelope (SASE). Follow this up by sending an article, flyer, brochure or promotional material that encourages a purchase. A mailing list compiled from classified responses could yield high numbers of orders. Code your ads to keep track of what works and what doesn't.

- **Direct Mail Advertising.** It is easier to sell books by direct mail if you can accurately identify and locate your audience or niche. Direct mail is quick to produce. With the correct list, offer and sales copy, direct mail can be a profitable way to reach your audience. Ask yourself: Is my product suitable to direct mail? Where can I advertise? Am I prepared to handle the incoming mail response, or should I use a fulfillment service? To determine the profitability of using direct mail, keep in mind that a 0-5% response rate is common. Associations and magazines generally rent the mailing list of their membership or subscribers. See *Encyclopedia of Associations* and *Standard Periodical Directory*.

> Before making a sizable investment in advertising, start small to test the effectiveness of your message. This way you can adjust your message until it yields the best results.

Check the legal regulations of mail order advertising in your state to follow the guidelines set forth by law. Write to the FTC and phone your State's Attorney General's office. Request information about complying with those regulations:

Federal Trade Commission (FTC)
Pennsylvania Ave & 6th St NW
Washington DC 20580
www.ftc.gov

- **Co-op mailing** is combining your mailer with someone else's and then sharing the expenses. This reduces your mailing costs, but dilutes your message. Co-op with someone whose product is compatible with yours, to reduce competing or conflicting messages.

*Half the money I spend on advertising is a waste;
the trouble is, I don't know which half.*
John Wanamaker

❑ **Mailing Lists.** Below are mailing list managers and brokers who specialize in renting targeted lists and address labels to book publishers. Request list types and pricing.

American Booksellers Association
828 S Broadway
Tarrytown NY 10591
(800) 637-0037
www.bookweb.org

American Business Lists
5711 S 86th Cr
Omaha NE 68127
(800) 336-8349
www.infousa.com

Open Horizons
P.O. Box 205
Fairfield IA 52556
(800) 796-6130
www.bookmarket.com

Para-Lists by Poynter
Box 8206
Santa Barbara CA 93118
(800) 727-2782
www.parapublishing.com

Promoting Your Book Online

The World Wide Web on the Internet is the most important new communication medium since television. It is a rapidly growing marketplace for the sale of books. Read *How To Publish and Promote Online* by M.J. Rose & Angela Adair-Hoy for an extensive list of ideas. The following are common ways to promote books online:

❑ **Web Site.** Having a website is the best way to provide information about your book via a computer. It acts as an introduction, to you, your book(s) and your publishing venture using a collection of information presented in words, sounds and images. A Web site can include your promotional programs, such as: new book announcements, news releases, book reviews, schedule of author appearances, excerpts, a graphic of a book's cover, ordering information and even links to services at other Web locations. When people visit your site, they may order, print or request additional information on your products or services. If you have purchased a Domain Name; Internet address through *networksolutions.com*, inquire about the cost and requirements to develop a web site through your "Internet Service Provider".

If you do not have a domain name, *Tripod.com* or *Geocities.com* offer inexpensive housing and easy to use templates to build your own website. Design your site with good content, articles, links and other useful information to attract visitors. The following company specializes in the development of Web Sites for book publishers:

The Bookzone
(460) 481-9737
www.bookzone.com

❏ **Promoting Your Web Site.** Establishing an Internet presence is not enough. An active promotional strategy to attract people to your site is essential. To make the most of this technology, an effective strategy might include:

• **Search Engines and Directory Listings.** Let the world know your site exists. An important way is to register your site in the online indexes that most people use to find things on the Web. Go to the top search engines and complete the registration form. Prepare in advance on your word processor the standard information required by Search Engines, then cut and paste the duplicate information when registering. Some top Search Engines and Directories are:

- Alta Vista   http://addurl.altavista.com
- Ask Jeeves   www.ask.com
- Dogpile   www.dogpile.com
- Excite   www.excite.com
- Google   www.google.com *(under directory tab)*
- Hotbot   www.hotbot.com/tools
- InfoMine   infomine.ucr.edu/participants/netgain.html
- Lycos   http://insite.lycos.com
- Yahoo   www.yahoo.com

www.submitplus.bc.ca offers a reasonably priced service submitting your site to search engines.

• **Reciprocal Links.** Exchanging links with other sites that attract the same audience is one of the most effective ways to direct people to your site and books. Send an email requesting an exchange. It's often easier to first establish a link to other sites, then email asking for a link to yours. Consider a "content link" which actually exchanges information such as an article or book cover with a purchase link to *Amazon.com*. Some search engines use the number of links to your site as a rating criteria; more links, the higher the rating. Periodically do a search, such as on *google.com,* to see who has listed you or your book.

❏ **Participating in Newsgroups & Mailing Lists.** Newsgroups and mailing lists are another way people with similar interests get together. When visiting a newsgroup, offer help in your area of expertise. Simply post an informative article by sending to any discussion group *(newsgroup)* or bulletin board *(BBS)* catering to your market niche. Mention that you would be glad to answer questions about your subject of expertise. Once you have established familiarity and trust, people will seek your advice. Be mindful of online etiquette when promoting your book. Check the FAQs (frequently asked questions), which are usually posted within each discussion/newsgroup, for do's and don'ts. Directories can be found at: *www.liszt.com, http://groups.google.com* and *http://groups.yahoo.com/.*

Mailing lists are a great way to meet and exchange emails with people who have similar interests. Anyone who is interested sends an email to a specific address, and then all the messages are sent to everyone on the list. Before subscribing, spend time getting acquainted with the list. Most mailing lists do not permit advertising. However, offering help or answering questions via email from interested parties supports a way to mention your book. Most email programs allow you to attach *a signature* or short blurb of information at the bottom of each email message. Keep your signature brief, mentioning your name, book title, website address and phone number. Most email programs allow you to create two or more signatures, thus it can be adjusted to different audiences. If your program does not have a signature capability, create a four or five line text file and cut and paste it on the bottom of every email you send.

❑ **Online Author Chats.** Book an event at various online chat groups. Approach the host like you would any media interview (page 50) tying your chat to current news or exciting information. This will increases the chance of a booking. Provide the host site material that will help promote your appearance, such as: blurbs, book cover, your picture, etc. Sites that host author chats:

- About.com   home.about.com/arts/index.htm
- American Online   www.aol.com
- Novel Talk   www.debstover.com/chat.htm
- Writers Write   www.writerswrite.net
- Wordsworth   www.wordsworth.com
- Yahoo.Com   chat.yahoo.com/?room=books@entertainment

❑ **Online Bookstore Reviews.** If your books are sold through online bookstores such as: *Amazon.com* or *Barnes and Noble.com,* encourage everyone you know to submit a favorable review of your book. In addition, review other books in your niche and mention in your attribution that you are author of (title of your book) and include your email address.

The shortest and best way to make a fortune in business is to let other people see it is in their interest to support yours.

❏ **Book Marketing Resources Online:**

• **Book Review Sources.** Database of book reviewers by subject category: www.bookzonepro.com/reviewers

• **Book Marketing Online.** Receive a free weekly book marketing update by sending an email to: majordomo@bookzone.com and type in the message area: subscribe bmu

• **PMA's Mailing List.** This is a forum of publishers who share ideas and answer questions for list mem bers. To join, send an email to: listserv@hslc.org and type in the message area SUBSCRIBE PMA-L along with your name.

• **Self-Publishing Resource Center by Wise Owl Books.** Useful articles, FAQs and a valuable links page: www.wiseowlbooks.com/publish

Writing is the only profession where no one considers you ridiculous if you earn no money.
Jules Renard

Shipping Books

❏ **Shipping & Mailing Books.** When shipping pallets of books, use national trucking lines listed in the phone book. They base their rates on shipping location, weight, and freight class. Paperback books have a different and less expensive freight class than the standard book class rate (class 60 versus 65 respectively). UPS ground offers a fine service for smaller quantities and offers a pickup service to contracted custom- ers. Single copies can be mailed most economically through the Postal Service at **Book Rate.**

The Post Office also offers **Priority Mail** at a bargain price compared to the overnight express service, if an extra day or two delay won't make a difference. Shipping expenses add up quickly. Managing postage and shipping costs is a good business practice. When mailing large quantities on a daily basis, the phone book lists mailing services which specialize in sending bulk quantities.

❑ **Discount Schedule and Policy.** Set a discount policy from the very start that is simple, clear and in writing so there is no misunderstanding. It is a requirement by the FTC that any discount you offer one type of dealer must be given to others who buy the same quantity. Your terms may differ when dealing with conventional channels of distribution as many work on a consignment basis only. Create a separate sheet of terms and discounts for Wholesalers, Bookstores and Special Direct Sales *(Alternative channels of distribution)* as standard discounts and terms differ for each. Include in your Terms and Conditions statement:

- Who pays the shipping and from where
- Breakdown of the quantity discount schedule
- Payment terms
- How to establish credit with you
- Return policy (if any)
- Special services such as *dropshipping & S.T.O.P.'s*

A Final Note. Publishing and promoting your own book can be an enriching experience. At times things will not run smoothly, and you will ask yourself: *"What did I get myself into?"* Some discouragement can be expected. Meet other self-published authors in your area to pool resources and share experiences. This can be a source of encouragement, a way to shorten learning time and an opportunity to combine promotional efforts. Welcome to the exciting world of publishing, and . . . **Good Luck!**

Subject Index

Index of Organizations and References

About The Author

Author, publisher and workshop leader **Mark Ortman** says; *"Getting my expectations bruised and learning the hard way have been my best teachers. Save yourself trouble by dreaming with your eyes wide open."* After receiving a Master's Degree in Communication from the University of Denver, Mark spent twelve years working in the training and development field. He was the recipient of ten national instructional awards for his inspiring teaching style. His published work includes: *Now That Makes Sense!, So Many Ways to Say Thank You, The Teacher's Book of Wit, A Simple Guide to Marketing Your Book* and the award-winning *Simple Guide to Self-Publishing.* He also plays keyboards and has composed *Wednesday's Dream*, an album of instrumental music. Mark lives in Bellingham, WA

Ordering Books

❑ *A Simple Guide to Self-Publishing* $10.95 US
❑ *A Simple Guide to Marketing Your Book* $10.95 US
~ Add $3.00 Shipping ~

Send check to:
WISE OWL BOOKS
Box 29205
Bellingham, WA 98228 USA
www.wiseowlbooks.com/publish

CPSIA information can be obtained
at www.ICGtesting.com
Printed in the USA
FSOW01n1232290216
17303FS